Leadership is Simple, Stupid!

You can keep your definitions of leadership for your beer circle. I don't care how you define it. If you want to do it, simply follow this checklist.

Table of Contents

Section 1 – Team Building

This section deals with the team you lead as a whole and your efforts to collect a disparate group of individuals into a whole whose sum is greater than its parts.

Chapter 1: People Inventory

First, inventory your people. You do not need to get to know them, the names of their spouses, kids and dogs. They don't frankly care if you remember their dogs' names. They care if you task them in a rational manner and the only way you possibly could do that is to know what they can do.

Inventory by Interview

Give your undivided attention to them and ask them a series of questions to find out their overall strengths and weaknesses, their academic/intellectual strengths/interests, their personality type, their teamwork/leadership experience, work experience, cultural/human and hobby experience.

Listen for Actionable Items

The purpose of this inventory is to place them in an appropriate role/position on the team. Listen for and question for details you need to decide how their skillset fits the mission. Think about how their potential/interests could fit the mission in the future with additional training/coaching or study. Ask about their interest in those roles and/or training.

Convert WIIFM to WIIFU

Teamwork is important for most teams. Ask specifically about a history of group experiences. This could be team sports experiences, community contributions, membership in volunteer groups, such as scouts, or anything that indicates an interest in groups or collections of people. WIIFM (What's In It For Me) is an anathema to teamwork. Collective self interest is the most effective way to work as a team. If we don't look good, one can't look good. Rarely do you have one singularly extraordinary member on an otherwise shabby team. Convert What's In It For Me to What's In It For Us.

Once you have a clear concept of the range and breadth of the employee, imagine where that person will fit into the mission now. Keep an eye out for how they might fit the mission in the future. Communicate that concept to the employee and ask for feedback. If the person says they can't do something, it's not mutiny; it's a data point. Adjust your concept of the individual's role according to the data points received in feedback. Communicate your overall intent for the employee and draw a clear picture that connects their tasks to the big picture of the company. Explain clearly why this task is important and how it is important. Ask if they understand and re-explain if necessary. Understanding their place in the total structure is critical to motivation and effective decision making on tasks when leadership isn't immediately available to answer a detailed question.

Note: If you are one of those leaders who believes your role is to squeeze every ounce of labor from an unwilling, innately lazy would be worker – the king of the coalition of the unwilling – then you are an idiot. This book can't help you.

Reality Check: People naturally want to succeed. Give them a chance, and they will. Shame and embarrassment are the most powerful human motivators, says Norbert Elias. Above all, no one wants to fail. You give them a chance to succeed by making a clear inventory of their unique and specific skills and matching those skills to the mission.

Nothing Motivates like Success

If you as a leader are effective at matching people's skillsets to specific projects, those projects will be successful. When those projects are successful, employees will feel comfortable.

Everyone hates to be overwhelmed and underemployed. Job satisfaction surveys on people who changed jobs indicated that most felt underemployed/unchallenged by the jobs they left. To effectively challenge an employee, task them at skillset +1. In fact, surveys have indicated that lack of challenge is one of the top reasons employees leave a company. This skillset + 1 system delegates responsibilities to them at a level above the skillset they currently have. While this will require more coaching and leadership on your part, it will result in a state of employment which is neither overwhelming nor boring.

People Hate Clockwatching

Sitting around staring at the clock and waiting to escape a Dilbert prison is a miserable experience. If as a leader, you can delegate tasks such that the employee feels engaged in the task to such a degree that the day flies by, then your employees will love you – even if you can't remember their spouse's name. Don't believe all that mushy garbage that has passed itself off as leadership theory in recent decades. Leadership is NOT about a relationship – mushy style – with people. It is about accurately matching skills to tasks. You can be the coldest fish in the company, but if you task your employees appropriately, they will love you.

Karl Marx was Wrong

The days of elementary school children working in dangerous jobs is gone for the first world. Mindless and manual jobs are increasingly done by machines and people do jobs that require brains. Perfect exploitation is a marvelous experience. To have a boss that knows exactly the talents and skills of the employee and assigns tasks perfectly matching those specific and humanly unique details to the projects and tasks the company needs done is like winning the lottery – the boss lottery.

Perfect Exploitation is Marvelous

Exploit perfectly the specific and unique talents and skills of each and every employee and they will love you, stay at your company and work harder and with more loyalty than any company could ask. Your job as a leader is to perfectly exploit every employee – that is to maximize the potential of their natural talents and traits, structurally reinforce any weaknesses by adding checks where necessary or augmenting their skills with training and cross training.

Know the Mission

All of this personal inventory theory is based on the idea that you know deeply and in detail the mission to be accomplished, the projects to reach objectives, and the in-the-grass details required to accomplish those objectives. If you don't, put this book down and find out. You can only match skills and talents to tasks if you know specifically what skills and talents are required to accomplish those tasks. If you don't have worker experience, try a few hours actually doing some of the tasks you need people to do. If that's impossible, observe employees doing the tasks. Get a deep, internalized grasp of the functions of your intended team.

Continual Improvement

Once you have inventoried every member of your team and assigned them tasks based on skillset +1, you'll need to continually adjust delegations according to personal growth. People are like streams, they are constantly moving. You must monitor their progress in talent and skill and upgrade delegation based on that growth.

Communications Failures are Yours

This is straight out of Sun Tzu's the Art of War. The leader and only the leader is responsible for failures in communication. If someone didn't understand what you said, you failed to state it in such a way that the information connected in a meaningful way with their mind/brain. The people inventory you did should be used to help you adjust your message to fit the recipient.

Chapter 2: Inventory Yourself

Second, inventory yourself. While you are talking with all your teammates, think about your skills in relationship to which skills are missing from your team. If you have skills you can use to fill in the missing gaps on your team, think about using your own skillsets to help train your team members with skills you need to accomplish the mission.

While you read this, you may be thinking where am I going to find time to do all this. Welcome to leadership. You should work harder, longer and with more focus, intensity and thought process than anyone on your team. That's leadership. Dare I say, "Suck it up?" It's not all bad. I love it when a plan a comes together.

The Head Shrink Stuff

If you haven't already realized that people are different, do try to learn this fact. Even when everyone looks the same, if they were to tell you everything about themselves, you'd find some were raised in rural, urban, suburban settings, some from lower, middle and upper middle, some from different religions or different branches of religion. This means they will all have different expectations, may have different criteria for what constitutes common sense, ethical boundaries, and appropriate language, personal space, invasion of privacy and a host of social norms.

This isn't an EEO course. Helping people feel comfortable with their differences and in many cases, admired because of their differences helps people perform at their respective peaks. Your job as a supervisor is to look for their maximum potential – to optimize them.

Introvert versus Extravert

If you're not already aware some people feel energized when interacting with others and some feel drained, do try to wrap your head around this. While only about 10% of us humans are truly introverted, do look for these people and ensure you try to keep them in their comfort zone. Likewise, don't try to put extraverts into silent, solo cubes. While trying to optimize people's performance, to the maximum extent possible try to adjust their environment and their tasks to their natural inclinations and talents.

Structure versus Freedom

Everyone fits someone on a continuum not only of introvert and extravert, but also of their comfort zones on structure and free, risk and safety, and a range of other dichotomies. As you inventory your teammates and yourself, think about all the members, yourself included on these ranges. Who requires more structure? Who requires more freedom?

As a supervisor, it's usually a relatively easy concept to give more structure. However, it can be time consuming. For those who need more structure, try to draft up Standard Operating Procedures that provide every step accounted for. If you have employees who need higher levels of structure, encourage them to participate in the process of drafting this kind of guidance.

While there is a risk, it can be rewarding to let employees who want more freedom to look for solutions to the work patterns themselves. In many cases, they can intuitively find more efficient methods of accomplishing the same tasks. If they have ideas, and if your company permits it, try to encourage them to seek out these options and document them. The documentation helps you maintain a modicum of control over the work and allows you to answer questions of more senior leaders. In fact, it is through this type of employees that companies often improve profit margins. It is more time consuming as a leader to work through new workflow concepts, but in the end, you may both come out looking better.

Encourage People to Change the Work Environment

Encouraging people either to improve the structure of their environment to suit their comfort zones or to explore more efficient options not only has the potential to improve corporate profit margins, it will go a long way toward employee retention.

All of this requires your effort, time, and focus. And the unfortunate reality is most leaders have a series of tasks they must complete – paperwork, reports, evaluations, interviewing potential new employees. Trying to organize all this on your schedule is no easy task. But it's worth the effort to do as much as you can to think about the individual employees' task-specific strengths and weaknesses, your task-specific strengths and weaknesses, the individual employees' personal comfort zones in structure, freedom, risk, risk management, intuitive improvement to work flow and personality types. The better you can understand how these factors play into the work's efforts, the better you can make leadership decisions.

Leadership Self Improvement

Even if you already have a university degree, if you've never taken psychology, sociology or cultural anthropology, you might think about taking these classes at a local community college or simply reading some audiobooks on these topics. Understanding the range and diversity of human experience can be a significant contributor to your understanding of the people on your team.

If your team lunches together or has coffee breaks today, listen to people's random chats and encourage them if they are interested in talking about themselves. You'll likely find that most of the people on your team occupy various subcultures. Subtle differences we don't think about – being Romanian-American, Korean-American, Irish-American or any other hyphenated category often brings with it a wide range of experiences that may be completely foreign to the leader even if we all live on the same block. People all have, to some extent, their own cultures.

ADD Adults

I often joke with colleagues that we all have attention deficit disorder. I don't know that that's true, but we all have a range of demands on our time. As most every job requires initial training and many jobs require ongoing training, understand how each of your employees learns. And understand how you learn best. This is a good question to ask people during the inventory interview.

Focus on people who learn by watching, doing, by reading or receiving lecture – in essence by concept, or any other method that works for them. Try to match instructions to the learning methods that fit the employees. This isn't always possible, but as leaders, we're looking to optimize people. So, whenever possible, do change a course from online computer learning to a classroom experience if the employee learns better in a traditional environment. If the employee is more conceptual or introverted by nature, try to arrange for online learning.

You may wonder why I put so much emphasis on learning. In the 21st century, technology is changing at an alarmingly rapid rate. If you company's techniques aren't changing; if you and your employees aren't looking for new software, freeware, shareware options and training employees to try new systems. Maybe you should be. A static company in this day and age might be headed for bankruptcy. So, look for new systems; train employees for those systems. Even if it's just for trial, encourage employees to try emerging technologies and to share their findings with the team.

Throw out "It's Okay to be Different"

This entire process of evaluation should be accomplished without opinion with regards to good or bad. It simply is. It's a factor. Like the hardness of stone or the strength of building materials, flexibility of plastic, etc. Evaluate people like you evaluate things in nature – scientifically. Categorize the specific characteristics without regard to how similar they are to you or to what you previously considered "normal."

Try to remove "normal" from your mind. Try to remove stereotypes, gender expectations, racial expectations from your thoughts. Again, this isn't an EEO course. Your mission is to optimize the use of the employee, so giving any kind of feedback like, "That's weird!" can reduce their willingness to share their insights. Some of the greatest teams in the world – like the team that created the Apple Computer, iPods and iPads were radically different from a demographic perspective. Try to throw out the book, It's Okay to be Different. It's isn't just okay, it's great!

Teams with people who look at things from various viewpoints can capitalize on the range and breadth of the experience of their members. They can not only get things done, they can often achieve things that less aware teams would be unable to accomplish. Leave your expectations at home and do your inventories of your self and your team without regard to your own life's history.

People who otherwise might not have a chance, like an immigrant or a person who has some kind of disability might be so eager to prove they are also capable that you'll find they are your best employees. Don't over look anyone. Focus on what they CAN do. Look for opportunities to capitalize on those skills and potential skills with a healthy disregard for traditional social expectations of limitation.

Broaden Your Mind

This chapter may seem like its all about others – introverts, training preferences, etc. It's not. It's about your understanding of people. That's why this chapter is called inventory yourself. This chapter is about your own perceptions of humans and expanding them to find the realities of the people on your team. Unless you studied ethnography abroad, chances are, your concepts of humans are remarkably narrow. You may have limited understanding or expectations of anyone you don't resemble. Look for the commonalities we all have, seek to understand the value in the very different approaches people take to their lives and work.

This isn't easy. Good Luck!

Chapter 3: Train Your Team as a Team

Third, train your team as a team.

Even if everyone in the entire organization knows his or her specific task — which is unlikely, they still need training in how their specific tasks interface with those of other members. This is where the whole exceeds the sum of the parts. In short, this is where the business can improve its profit margin and leaders earn their value, making their greatest contribution.

Look for synergistic pairs

Having inventoried all members and established clearly in your mind strengths and weaknesses of every member, look for pairs that can shore up weaknesses. Now, you move beyond individual capabilities and you look for pairs or small groups of people, which if combined, would alleviate some blind spots in people's skills and minds. This could include pairing someone with a kind of personal coach, but it might include pairing different personality types.

A Brief Example

I'm an action person by nature or perhaps by Marine Corps training. One of my colleagues in Japan was a series academic thinker. Our boss had a couple of problems. The thinker never moved or acted on his concepts. Sometimes I moved too quickly without sufficient contemplation for future or alternative consequences. He figuratively sewed us together. As a team, we drove each other nuts. I couldn't stand his continual rambling. He felt my single-digit word count communications weren't sufficiently nuanced.

While the experience was psychologically uncomfortable for both of us, the boss explained in clear detail why we were being paired. He joked about my binary brain. I noted the two of us were hard-wired differently. And my side kick noted that he would never have used a phrase like hard-wired to describe people. I'd tell him, "Okay you have 10 minutes to philosophize on this topic. Then, regardless of where you brain is, we're going to decide and act." I tried really hard to listen to ramblings to actionable items. The end result was that all of the projects for both us were qualitatively better than either one of us had previously achieved.

More than the Sum of the Parts

These synergistic pairs should make both parties more capable than either one ever would have been singly. Identify not only a pair of employees, but also a task that the specific and unique talents of each will be effectively exploited if jointly applied. Communicate your concept to both of them together and give them both an opportunity to contemplate and respond to your vision. Adjust your vision based on their collective feedback. This is a trial and error process. Don't worry if early attempts don't work, just keep swinging.

Having established synergistic small teams of two or three, pair those sets together into teams of five or so people. Continue collecting teams until you find, through trial and error, the perfect core team size for your operation. In the U.S. Marine Corps, a core team is five, a fire team. However, I saw a highly effective operation in Korea that was centered around five Americans and 12 Koreans for a total of 17 per core team. The specific number is flexible and largely depends on the function. The bottom line is to divide and conquer large numbers of employees by put them into manageable teams.

No Sage on the Stage

You don't have to be the smartest one in the room. Amputate your ego. You do have to have the best judgment in the room. Judge ideas, not people. When employees bring ideas to you, you must be able to effectively evaluate that idea. You and you alone decide if the idea should move forward and you and you alone take responsibility for its failure. The success of any idea, of course, belongs to the employee who dreamed it up. Narcissistic CEO is Hitler-ized crap. Don't make yourself the center of your universe, people will hate you. Recognize their unique and specific talents and ideas and capitalize on them. The only thing that matters is project/mission success. You make the mission happen. You and all your employees are subordinate to the collective self-interest of successful collaborative projects.

Hitch the Mules to the Cart

Having established synergistic core teams, step back and evaluate all of their projects/efforts. I can't tell you how many times I've seen one core team moving in one direction and another core team in the same company/organization moving in an opposite direction. No human, no matter how stupid would hitch mules to opposite ends of the same cart and wonder why the cart doesn't move. Sadly leaders often do not synchronize the efforts of their own employees. Make sure the efforts of the teams complement each other rather than strangle each other.

Nick the New Guy Disruption

Every time you get a new guy, evaluate his skills and adjust the entire team according to his unique and specific talents and skills. If he has strengths that his predecessor didn't have, you may want to move tasks from another to him. Additionally, if he has weaknesses that his predecessor didn't have, you may want to pair him with someone to coach him or move that task to someone else.

Storming!

I assume you already know the 1965 Bruce Tuckman theory of forming, storming, norming and performing. Some people forget that whenever a team gets a new member, which in the 21st century is surprisingly frequent, the entire team goes back to the forming stage. Keep this in mind when Nick the New Guy comes in. Adjust synergistic pairs, teams, processes, projects according to the incoming talent/skills. Also, if you haven't already read Bruce's book, do take a look. It's one of the truly great management pieces in human history.

Chapter 4: Delegation is Training

Fourth, make a training plan for everyone incorporating all members, elements of the mission and include yourself. Training is continuous. Once you know the unique and specific talents of each employee, develop an individual development plan with each person.

Delegate at Skillset +1

As already mentioned, delegated tasks should be assigned at a level of skillset +1. How can a person accomplish tasks they don't currently have the skillset for? In addition to the delegation, you have to determine, in coordination with the employee what training they need to accomplish the task. In some cases, this could be as simple as Googling guidance and following it. In other cases, it could be enrolling in a master's degree program. To a large degree, this element is dependent on how motivated the employee is to take on education and training.

You can compromise and allow some work time for research and understanding, but in many cases, the employee will need to read books, enroll in courses, and expand their lives. Making this determination is a highly interactive process and the employee is in the driver's seat. That's okay. You the leader, do not always have to drive. In fact, you'll find that many employees, once you remove the reigns, will amaze and inspire you. And that's awesome.

Look for training opportunities within your organization and within your own teams. Pair people together as coach and student. This will be a good training experience for the coach as well as for the student as it helps the coach learn leadership skills. Cross training is a great way to keep a team flexible both in people's individual talents and in tasks. An effectively cross-trained team will hardly notice vacations/sick time or unexpected absences of members because alternative members are already fully versed on secondary and tertiary tasks.

Training Takes Time

As a leader, you need to plan for and allot time for training. This will be challenging as the daily operations will likely eat up all the time on the schedule. Bite the bullet and do it anyway. One thing to be carefully and consciously aware of: Nick the New Guy needs training before he will be useful.

Most organizations that are expanding have task-saturated teams. They think hiring or bringing in new people will solve the problem. It will not. New members actually increase the burden on the team when they first arrive. They must be trained. They don't know the tasks, the company culture, the team members, or their place on the team. New people require more attention and effort from a team. Wherever possible, do not add members to task saturated team. Add members BEFORE the team becomes overwhelmed. Anticipating shortfalls before they happen is northing short of a miracle, but do try to live by the adage: Never underestimate your enemies, never overestimate your team.

Roll up Your Sleeves and Get into the Fight

Push the schedule around and if necessary, take over some employee tasks yourself, so members can get training and expand skills. I've been so impressed with very high ranking leaders who did menial tasks including answering phones and other reception work at critical moments in a team's development. Similarly, most restaurant managers know this well, as many of them, if they are good, have washed dishes when the dishwasher didn't come to work. Restaurant managers routinely cook, clean tables, take orders and act as cashiers. This leadership flexibility shouldn't be limited to restaurants. All leaders need to take up the difference between employees' capabilities and project demands.

Delegation is training because assigning an employee to do a task she cannot already do will give her an opportunity to grow. The task should be slightly above the level of skill of the employee, ensuring this will challenge the employee. If you are able to significantly expand the employee's skillset, especially to a level they themselves never conceived possible, you will have a deeply loyal and hard-working employee. You can improve retention, reduce hiring/head-hunting costs and overall improve the company's bottom line.

Some People are Stupid

Sometimes the stupid person will be you. However, some of your employees will shock you with stupidity. You have two choices. You can spend a lot of time working on legally removing them from the equation. This can be challenging. Or you can look for a place where they might fit into the team. Option 2 is at least worth examining.

We have to be honest with ourselves. Humans are generally intelligent animals, but talent is not evenly distributed. You will have an employee who doesn't live up to your expectations. Lower your expectations. See if you can adjust the team to accommodate a new role for them. If you can, you can save yourself the trouble of firing them, providing the salary paid is appropriate to the tasking, you'll be better off. If you can't, sometimes there's no other option but to remove an employee. Nonetheless, relocation, if possible, can save you time and the company money. Consider the possibilities.

Summary

Up to this point, all leadership tasks have been connected. Inventory the employee skill set and talents to effectively form synergistic pairs and form those into small teams. Using the people inventory, ensure communications are shaped in terms they understand. Using the people inventory, determine assignments based on skill sets +1 and formulate an agreed upon development/training plan for each person to help them reach the skills necessary to successfully accomplish the challenging delegations you've given them.

Chapter 5: Collective Self Interest

Fifth, understand the value of looking good as a unit, as a team. Communicate that value to your naturally individualistic employees – which would be everyone. As humans, we learn first to cry as infants to get our own needs met. Theoretically, upon reaching adulthood, we learn to play with others in the sandbox. Yeah, not so much.

Everyone wants to shine. The trouble is, rock stars often dampen the energy and effort of people who are still developing. From a team project perspective, by undermining the growth of less skilled players, those with more self-confidence or downright arrogance will ultimately undermine the total potential of the team.

Look at your team from the perspective of your headquarters. Most likely the highest levels of your organization don't even know your name or the names of your employees and possibly don't even know your section's name. The way the whole unit moves up in recognition is by optimizing all the players.

Adam Smith was Wrong

Remember the movie, *A Beautiful Mind*, where the lead character lays out plan so all the frat boys can get lucky? They all want the tall blond. But the brilliant mathematician realizes if they all go for the tall blond, she'll spurn them all. They'll go for her friends 2nd and they'll feel like 2nd best. So those girls will spurn them all. In short Sun Tzu's approach to giving awards only to the fastest gladiator (warrior) doesn't work. In the movie, *A Beautiful Mind*, he says suddenly, "Adam Smith was wrong."

Adam Smith was one of the earliest and brightest minds in economics. He believed that an economy, like ours, would be most effective if it were driven by enlightened self-interest. However, the problem with the pure self-interest driven economy was the exploitation of early factories. John Nash realized that Adam Smith got it half-right. Collective self interest is the most effective structure for an economy, society and even for a five-man team. Make the entire team more effective, individually more skilled and more interactive and interdependent. The whole team will look good to senior leadership. This means the leader of that team looks good and members of that team are more likely to win individual awards.

Compare the collective self-interest driven team to a purely individualistic team. Occasionally someone might rise above the din of daily work to show their brilliance, but on the whole, most are condemned to a life of drudgery. Such teams may fall into cliques, talking about each other, perhaps even backstabbing one another. The overall feeling is hostile and uncomfortable and leaves members wondering how long they might be employed. Not performing at their relative peaks or contributing in a valuable way to the organization or mission, they feel underemployed and mentally unengaged in the tasks at hand. In short, they are likely to move on if a more inviting corporate environment seems probable or even mildly possible.

Trust is Critical

An effective collective self-interest driven team must have trust among its members and this starts with leadership. It's well known that one of the best ways to get someone to confess something is to establish a good rapport and then disclose something personal. Having made yourself vulnerable, it is now easier for the other to make himself or herself vulnerable because they have a kind of socio-psychological upper hand.

Be a Brutally Honest Leader

Set the tone for verbal honesty by telling your employees as much information as you are permitted by corporate rules and as time permits. Most of all, if/when you screw up, tell the employees immediately. And tell them how you will remedy your miscalculation. By setting this kind of tone yourself, you can develop an environment where people are more likely to be honest with you in a one-on-one environment. You can slowly expand this by being open and surprisingly honest in group discussions and you'll likely find that others will follow your behavior, sharing honestly in the group. You develop an environment where people are willing and able to tell others about their failed attempts.

There are NO Failures

A zero-defect mentality reduces employees' willingness to risk attempts and undermines their willingness to talk openly about the chances for success or failure of a given concept. Allow an environment were its okay to try and fail. Allow yourself and your teammates to take some risk and report back what they learned about that attempt – what it indicates may be effective on a subsequent try and what it indicates likely wouldn't be worth further investigating.

As with the earlier "no judgments" on people's specific learning preferences, personality types, unique personal histories, comfort zones for structure and freedom, risk and risk management, do no judge the attempts by their failures. Do judge attempts by how rational the connection between the proposed action and a possible solution are. However, the fact that an attempt failed is not a point for positive or negative judgment, only analysis.

Independent Trust

Have you ever sat through one of those absurd corporate offsite "trust training" adventures? Where you have to cross your arms and close your eyes and fall backward and let the next employee prevent you from falling to the ground. Did you get anything out of that? Yeah, not so much.

You know you need your employees to trust each other, depend on each other and invest in each other. The question is how to do that? I love the way the Marines did it in the 1980s, but don't try this at your office. One Marines shows up in a crumpled uniform and the sergeant yells at the guy next to him telling him he's responsible for his teammates and if not, he'll get us all killed. Inattention to detail gets people killed in combat!!!   Okay, that's not going to work in Dilbert-ville, although it might work on an oil rig.

Instead, make people actually responsible for each other. The earlier mentioned synergistic pairs – from Chapter 2 – one of those two people is likely to be the trainer/coach. You'll spell out for him how his ability to guide and train this person will be/can be noted in his evaluation as a commentary on his mentoring/leadership skills. Whenever possible, look for an opportunity to point out how people impact one another's work.

Look For the Assist

Nobody makes a score without reinforcements. Be sure to note those reinforcing elements, teams and people by name at corporate events. This could be something as simple as a weekly meeting. Praise not only for getting ball down the field, but to those who blocked, ran, threw and caught. Illustrate when you give due credit that virtually every success takes a team.

Interdependent units create a natural development in professional trust over time – without the expensive and cheesy offsite training.

No Cliques

As a leader, be careful to watch for the development of cliques. This is different from synergistic pairs or other highly functional sub units. A clique culture is one in which subgroups are vying against one another for leadership attention. When done in a positive mood, casual competition can add spice and excitement to the work environment. The problem happens when people are coming to you with concerns about someone else's problem.

Built-in Lie Detector

Look constantly for signs of a lack of integrity. If people are bringing you legitimate professional concerns, that's okay. If people are bringing you gossip, you have a problem. The way to reduce backstabbing in a unit is: do not respond to gossip – in a psychological sense, put the behavior on extinction (See Pavlov).

However, you can only do this if you are aware that you're being played.

Remember the culture of the corporation you live in is largely determined by how people's behavior is reinforced or discouraged. As a leader, you want to be careful to encourage positive behaviors that improve functionality of people, teams and processes. Likewise, you want to strongly discourage behavior that debilitates a team.

When an employee brings you a piece of information about another employee who is causing them problems, ask yourself, "Why is this person telling me this information?" The first answer and sometimes the right answer is they genuinely care about the team. However, don't let that be the end of your mental interrogation. Is there some reason this person wants another person to look bad? Is there something the speaker has to gain from any loss of favor from leadership the "problem person" might experience as a result of the conversation with leadership? Does the information seem consistent? Of course, all data points should be evaluated on this criterion.

Why People Lie

There is an amazing array of reasons people lie and not all of them are relevant to any investigation. People lie to be polite. They lie to avoid embarrassment. Understand that evaluating someone's integrity is based purely on whether a modification of information has malicious intent. Saying the weather is lovely with a wry smile while it's storming outside is clearly not a factual statement, but neither is it a violation of integrity. Developing a clear understanding of integrity is essential for leadership and it's challenging.

Going back to ethnographies – if you can study some foreign cultures and how they use truthful and untruthful statements in daily discourse, it could help you step out of your stereotypes about how people "should" communicate. This can help you better evaluate the integrity of people's statements and better adjust your statements to fit the unique and specific subculture of your corporation.

No Randians

Ayn Rand was a Russian writer in the 1960s obsessed with power and the then subservient role of women and she argued that no one had an obligation to serve anyone else. In fact, by the 1980s, what Rand described would become known as personality disorder known as codependency. While those who read her actual works didn't develop the concept that self-obsession is a rational right, their children often did. Absorbing their parents ideas during family conversations without full processing the philosophy behind it, they became nightmarishly convinced they should look out for #1. Anything else is irrational. This kind of justified selfishness inhibits effective collective work and is nearly impossible to reason around or beyond.

If it were up to me, I'd screen every employee for hints of Randian principles and hire only those who did not harbor such concepts. Working together requires a certain level of selflessness and building a team with people who think selfishness is reasonable is nearly impossible.

Team Sports

The opposite of Randians tend to be people who play team sports. This may, at first seem like an odd discussion for professional development. However, when I was promoted to the rank of corporal in the Marine Corps, I asked my former collegiate football player captain how I could become a better leader. He recapped that my high school sports had been wrestling, track and cross country. I didn't see the relevance, but agreed with the facts presented. You've always participated in individual sports, he noted. Join a sports team.

While I really couldn't see the relevance, I obeyed and on the first day of soccer practice, I got it. The coach asked us to memorize each other's names and call out our positions vis-à-vis one another. I became consciously aware of my position on the field in relationship to other members.

Whenever you see an opportunity in your company to permit your team members to use company time to do team sports or community volunteer work, you should. This will significantly improve your team's performance over time.

Section 2 – Leadership Responsibilities

While it's highly probable you're feeling overwhelmed from the laundry list of details you must attend to with the first section, this focuses more on the specific responsibilities of leadership with a special eye to how bad leadership or the complete lack of leadership can result in failures.

Chapter 6: Take Responsibility, Share Credit

Always remember that everyone is watching everything you do.

Set the Example; Lead by Example

If you come in late to work or late to meetings on a regular basis, you have tacitly set the standard by which all employees will measure themselves and their peers. If this is the environment you intend – maybe early Google years when the development of search technology was more important than timeliness, particularly as employees routinely worked through the nights, weekends, meal breaks with little regard to punching a time clock – this is okay.

Be conscious that your standards – of integrity, such as lying to a friend regarding why you can't come to lunch – sets the standards for your subordinates. They watch everything you do. When you set a double standard, you can be sure they are talking about it with enthusiasm and interest.

Most importantly, when you err, confess it. We talked about this earlier, but this point can't be stressed enough. Your integrity sets the standard for your team.

Try Not to Generate Ideas

Yes, you're the boss, so your ideas are supreme. How boring! However, if you pitch ideas, you'll be likely to think they are the best, bias being what it is.

To be objective, it's better not to pitch ideas. Rather pitch problems to the team, let them develop various proposals for courses of action and let them vote on those courses of action.

If it looks like their agreed upon ideas will accomplish the intended goals, suppress the impulse to jump in and recommend or decide.

To the maximum extent possible, let people run themselves. This is, of course, depending on where they are in the Forming, Storming, Norming and Performing cycle. Avoid the impulse to dictate to your unit.

The only time you should jump in is when the team asks for your assistance – expresses confusion over a problem and indicates a lack of ideas for resolving the problem. Even in that case, wherever possible, just ask questions and see if you can lead them – inspire them to generate their own solutions.

Praise Publically

Once the team has come up with the solution, worked it through and completed the project, praise publically, giving specific credit to team members you observed in key roles.

Make Timely Decisions

If any team is waiting on clearance from you, from more senior leadership or from lateral sub teams, try to get that determination as quickly as possible. Few things kill the momentum of a unit like sitting around waiting to begin work.

As a leader, your job is to remove obstacles from the path of progress. However, in many organizations, the clearance process becomes a debilitating obstacle. This is not to say that clearance in and of itself is bad. In fact, in many cases, critical inputs come in from other key players. The data points from the clearance process are highly conducive to a successful project. Just pay close attention that the time required to get those clearances is reasonable. In most cases, junior personnel aren't able to push a clearance. As a leader, this is one of your responsibilities. Keep a record of pending clearance requirements and once they have been delayed a day, give a friendly call and ask what's taking so long.

Make sure subordinates know you have defined this as one of your responsibilities and encourage them to come to you if a clearance or approval is holding up progress.

Failure of any Project is Yours Alone

Never blame subordinates for project failures. Subordinates are responsible only for their own individual failings – such as the failure to arrive on time. However, the collective work of any team is the sole responsibility of the team leader. This may understandably seem like an inherent contradiction. Earlier, we discussed avoiding the impulse to dictate to your unit. I urged you not to propose solutions, and wherever possible to encourage teams to make collective decisions on their own. Now, you get stuck holding the stinking bag of …. You know.

Yes, leadership maintains credibility of subordinates and keeps morale high by not crushing failures. Failure is its own crush. There's no need to further discuss it. Representing the failure as your own to senior leadership endears your team members to you because they know exactly where the failures occurred.

However, blaming them and exonerating yourself can create a serious chasm between you and the team. Don't think the comments you made to leadership will be held in confidence. Such expectations of secrecy will ultimately be shared through paths you didn't know existed and will ultimately come back to haunt you.

Take the hit for the team. Give a speech about regrouping and encourage everyone to collectively try again. Also go back through the skills and training evaluation of each individual and synergistic pairs. If you've done your homework right before this point, you should never have faced failure to begin with.

Chapter 7: Communicate

Evaluate every piece of information that comes across your eyes and consider who needs to see it. As you are undoubtedly experiencing data overload in the 21st century, try to keep in mind that your subordinates, peers, and seniors are having the same experience. Share only the data that you think each person needs to know. Work to develop a similar communication ethic among every member of your team.

Follow Through on Follow Up

While determining which data is useful to who can be challenging, one determination is easy: follow-through. If anyone has asked you for something, communicate with them the status of that request. First, communicate that the request was received. Then, at each step in the process be sure to share the results with them.

Ensure your subordinates provide this kind of feedback to projects you assign them and ensure you provide this kind of feedback up the chain and laterally within your organization.

Keeping employees in the dark breeds rumor mills. Rumors are almost always unproductive, not only because of the time wasted in proliferating rumors, but also because of decisions employees make from the inaccurate information in rumors. Even if you don't have complete data, whenever possible share corporate information with team members. Even if you have legally binding obligations like unions, this openness with regards to legitimate corporate data will serve you well, maintaining a positive and open communication environment between employees and leadership and among members on the team.

Expecting people to make effective, rational decisions given a dearth of valid data is an unreasonable expectation. Keep your employees informed at all times of all elements of projects or working conditions that are relevant to their sectors of responsibility.

Who Serves Who Anyway?

If it's beginning to feel like you serve your employees, not the other way around, then you're getting the gist of this book. If they don't look good, you don't look good – yes, I stole that from the Vidal Sassoon commercial.

Doing great work requires effective intervention from leadership. Sitting around reading the newspaper doesn't make a smooth running operation. Leadership is continuously hard work. "Taking care of the troops" isn't just a platitude; it's an effective means of operation. The problem is that most people don't actually know what it means. It doesn't mean memorizing spouse names. It does mean ensuring they have whatever they need to accomplish the task at hand.

So often I have looked at a task and the means to accomplish it and reflected on biblical stories about people being robbed of straw while trying to make brick. Or better yet, of the red ball video, a small piece of Total Quality Leadership/Management from the 1970s/80s.

Red Ball Video

In this video, a mock employee is urged to produce more white balls, which are captured on the end of a drilled wooden old school principal's paddle. Scooping through a large bucket of red and white balls, the "employee" has zero control over the color of the balls that will land on the paddle.

Too often, the structure of work assigned is analogous to this video. Employees are held accountable for results they have no way to control. I still love this video, although I haven't been able to locate it in a few years.

As a leader, you need to think about the structure of the work environment – the equipment, training, the sequence of events, the clearance procedures, the approval procedures and ask if these are logical, linear or effective. Your job is to make sure the tasks are completed. This is only possible if the employees are given the means to accomplish the tasks.

Ensure the task is understood

One element of communicating and leading is making absolutely sure the task is understood. This may seem like the obvious, but employees often don't want to appear stupid, so may not ask questions. As the leader, you've most likely been at the organization longer, have a deeper background on the reason for the task, and probably attend a range of meetings that provide you a wealth of data the employee has never contemplated. Try to look at the world through the eyes of someone who doesn't have your experience. What do they need to know?

As such, when you assign a task, make a conscious effort to include a full background on the topic – a who, what, when, where and why approach. This may seem like overkill, but in your absence, you'll want the employee to be able to adjust to changing conditions and achieve the end result you would have wanted if you were available for them to question.

SMEAC

Marines and other military use SMEAC – Situation, Mission, Execution, Administration/Logistical requirements and Communication/Command and Control. Undoubtedly for anyone not in the military, this sounds scary, especially the part about executing.

In fact, the who, what, when, where and why approach is quite similar. Situation – what are the conditions? Mission – What are we doing? Execution – Just Do It – or how are you going to do it? Administrative/Logistical – what kind of paperwork is necessary? Does something have to be moved, acquired to do it? Communication – who should I tell about it and when?

Regardless of what kind of checklist you use to give a task, it's a good idea to run through a checklist in your head every time you give an employee a task. Give them a full understanding of the task, not just the bare essentials.

Questions are Great

Encourage subordinates to ask questions concerning any point in your instructions they do not understand. It's an unfortunate reality of new or insecure leaders that they feel questions are questioning their ability or authority. On the contrary, questions for clarity are great.

Questions show that employees are paying attention and are genuinely trying to ensure they can accomplish the task adequately. Even if questions are from someone who is trying to challenge your authority, respond to them as if they were simply a question.

Always remain focused on the task and try to ensure that everyone knows exactly what they're trying to do. Keep a level of detachment from needling team members. Putting the behavior on extinction often serves you well. See Pavlov for more guidance on putting behavior on extinction.

Faulty Tasking Results in Faulty Completion

I once asked an injured recruit on temporary assignment to the headquarters to continue making multiple copies of the last item he copied the evening before. (Note: in some cases, service members unfit to train will be placed on easy duties until they are healed sufficiently to return to training.) Of course, the LAST item he copied the evening before was a single copy of the commander's annual leave papers (permission to go on vacation).

Of course, I didn't need 20 copies of the commander's annual leave papers. I needed 20 copies of the press release I was going to hand out that day at the local military museum.

As an entry level service member still in recruit training, it's highly probable that he'd never seen annual leave papers before. As a teen just out of high school, it's equally likely he'd never seen a press release. It was completely unreasonable for me to expect he'd know the difference between the two documents he was tasked to photocopy.

Without sufficient context for a given task, it is irrational to expect employees to accomplish that task effectively and efficiently. Enough said.

Chapter 8: Develop a Bird's Eye View

This might well be the most difficult task you must accomplish; you've got to step back from the work and see it from a holistic perspective.

Unless you went to one of the academies and immediately out of college took over a company of military service members, chances are you spent some time as an employee before you became a leader. You developed a habit of looking at tasks from the grassroots' perspective.

So, how do you suddenly soar up to look at the grass from the tree line? Any cognitive shift is challenging. However, there might be a few drills that could help. While you try to think of your team and its functions in relationship to other teams and their functions, try doing some of the tasks you didn't previously do.

Doing more grassroots tasks may seem like an illogical approach to developing a broader view, but your understanding of a range of tasks will likely give you insight as to how they work together.

Quality Assurance Problem

I took a lot of heat in South Korea for doing some of the manual labor tasks of our local staff. However, as I sat beside the local team, chatting and doing the manual labor, I noticed that one machine was particularly problematic. I had to run a given product through it two or three times on average and occasionally as many as five times.

I asked my Korean colleagues if this was normal and they said unfortunately, it was for this machine. They said that three or four Americans ago they had brought it to someone's attention, but were told it wasn't significant. The other 8 units' machines generally worked on the first run, they told me.

I brought this to the attention of senior leadership and they called a technician to have the alignment checked. Turned out that while ours was the worst, three of the eight machines were well beyond the appropriate tolerance for quality assurance.

In the first section, I said if you don't know the mission, put down this book and figure it out. That said, your understanding of the purpose of your company and its products will likely deepen and broaden the longer you serve in a leadership role. Maintain a constant curiosity and try continually to connect the dots – that is see relationships between various functions and elements of the company.

Lunch Around

Have lunch with ever subordinate, with a secretary in every office and with as many peers as possible. This option might not be appropriate depending on how rumors run in your office, but one of my previous colleagues said it worked very well for him.

Each lunch should be one-on-one and you should only talk shop. Try to see the company through the eyes of the person you are lunching with. I can imagine this might seem odd if you've been working at a company for a decade or two. You probably think you already know everything about the company.

Try to open your mind to the idea that there are a lot of areas of responsibility outside your purview. As an employee, those areas weren't critical to your performance, however, as a leader, your ability to swallow the elephant whole – that is to comprehend the company in its entirety and see your unit's place in that whole is valuable.

Brief Death

Death by PowerPoint is a common phrase for military and government personnel and it generally means sitting through a really boring presentation where the presenter simply reads everything on the slide in front of you. What makes these fleetingly fatal moments tolerable is the Mystery Science Theater experience that is usually provided by a couple of sarcastic shadows in the dark room, adding a Rocky Horror Picture Show like second dialogue to an otherwise banal diatribe.

The only thing worse than Death by PowerPoint is to dig up those briefs and read through them in the comfort and silence of your office without the pain relieving comic commentary. Sadly, that's exactly what I recommend you consider doing. If you can tolerate it, this can help you deepen and broaden your understanding of your company's function and the role of your team within that paradigm.

Share Your Ideas

While on your quest to better understand your unit's place in the greater company picture, share your observations. Start with your subordinates first. See if they agree with what you see. Adjust your ideas according to their insights. Share your ideas with your peers. And lastly, share them with your leadership.

Listen attentively for ideas and insights you can use to adjust your perspective. Note: If the response to your observations is silence – crickets chirping – you might have missed the mark. Go back and re-inventory. Of course, it might be that neither your peers nor your leadership have ever thought about the company holistically. Sadly a complete lack of leadership is unreasonably common. We've got to generate those reports, ya know?

Too often leadership, like employees, are task saturated and obsessed with completing a series of tasks, often whose relationship to the company's function, they don't understand.

Chapter 9: Get Wrench-turner's Grip

Now that you've got your bird's eye view, let's get back in the weeds.

Management Sucks

This morning I went to have a classic American breakfast – eggs and bacon, pancakes and hash browns. I love American breakfast. I overheard my waiter telling his colleagues he wanted to take a job at a different greasy spoon. "Why?" they asked. "It will only be the same as here."

"Yes, except that the refrigerator door might not be broken, so items near the door might not be spoiled. They might keep their inventory in stock so when I reach for a bottle of hot sauce, it's there. I might actually be able to serve customers."

His colleagues laughed in lively manner and said, okay, you have a point.

How could his management be so truly clueless? Or better yet, how could the management so many of us have worked for have been so truly clueless.

Let's take a closer look at what happens when the "Us and Them" mentality takes over management and employees.

Suddenly Stoic

During one of the many "Death by PowerPoint" presentations I endured in the Marine Corps, I was assigned to observe a group solving problems as part of a Total Quality Leadership drill in the early 1990s.

A major, a lieutenant, a master sergeant and two staff sergeants sat around a table to discuss a problem. The major did most of the talking. The lieutenant's primary contribution was to agree with the major. The master sergeant did a reasonable amount of talking, but one of the staff sergeants' contribution to the group discussion was a head nod. The other made only one comment.

If I hadn't seen it with my own eyes, I wouldn't have believed it. I've always believed Marines were bold – willing to say the truth, sometimes hard truths to leadership.

To be fair, it could be that the staff sergeants had categorized this as Death by PowerPoint and had mentally checked out, while the leadership was trying to at least pretend to play along with the role play. Fair enough.

Still, it stuck in my head. Subordinates often don't speak in front of leadership. We leaders and managers need to draw them out.

We're Only Bitchin'

Leadership by walking around is a rather famous military style and it's remarkably effective. You get a good view of what's happening and people talk to you – about just about anything. In fact, employees talk openly in a way they would never talk if they went to your office. Face it – people only come to your office to tell you something when the sky is falling. But talking to the boss when he's strolling or smoking a cigarette, that's just jiving.

So, be careful what you ask for. You need information from the all levels of organization, but when you stay in your office, no one tells you anything and when you walk around, all they do is bitch. It's too hot on the flight line. Really? Did you think the leadership could turn down the sun over a North Carolina summer?

So you go from getting nothing to getting a tsunami of chatter with nothing of value. What you really need is actionable items. Like the information at the beginning of this chapter – about low stocked items, broken equipment, and other mission failure data points. Like a whale sifting water for plankton, you need to sift through all the verbal garbage going by you and find the issues that genuinely require your attention. The answer is the man who turns the wrench is the best one to tell you if it fits the bolt.

Japanese War Machine Revolutionized America

According to the business management history as it's told in Wikipedia, W. Edwards Deming "made a significant contribution to Japan's later reputation for innovative high-quality products and its economic power. He is regarded as having had more impact upon Japanese manufacturing and business than any other individual not of Japanese heritage."

I see things a little differently.

Deming was an otherwise unremarkable manager who went to Japan after WWII, made observations about things like a continual improvement cycle and reported those observations in books. I love books like *Dr. Deming: The American Who Taught the Japanese about Quality*. Can you say pure grade bull?

Immediately following Pearl Harbor, the Japanese Navy took a strategic objective every day for more than 7 consecutive days, running through Pacific islands like a hot knife though butter. At the beginning of World War, the Japanese air force destroyed Douglas MacArthur's entire air force on the ground in the Philippines. That act that engendered the ultimate fall leading to the Bataan Death March. Those were dark days for American military.   The bottom line is, the Japanese knew something about manufacturing, steel and quality a long time before Dr. Deming arrived on stage.

I think Dr. Deming simple packaged the Japanese methodology for export and transported it to the U.S. where his ideas did have a positive impact on U.S. manufacturing. I'm dubious as to whether he had any impact on Japanese manufacturing. Regardless, his ideas or the Japanese ideas translated and packaged by him, have merit.

One of the most critical concepts is the man turning the wrench is the best one to tell you if it fits the bolt. This is an extension of a sociology/cultural anthropology concept that all knowledge is local. But, what exactly does that mean?

Barefoot, Illiterate Farmers are Brilliant

As an example: during the Great Leap forward in China, the Chinese government though they could supercharge their economy and rapidly industrialize through central planning. They created one of the greatest manmade disasters on earth resulting in estimates in the tens of millions of deaths due to starvation. In addition to redirecting labor and efforts from farming toward steel production, central planners told regional farms which crops to produce. As micro-climates, soil types and a range of factors effect which crops grow best in which fields, central planners couldn't possibly know better than barefoot, illiterate local farmers what works.

Why this is important to leaders? You need to have a very Socratic understanding of knowing what you don't know. In the text Socrates Defense (Apology), he questions one expert after another looking for someone wiser than himself. However, he finds that all so-called experts, while they do have some specific knowledge, presume themselves to have a wider range of information than they actually do. In fact, they themselves do not know the limits of their own information. Socrates concludes simply to know what you don't know makes a person remarkably wise vis-à-vis their peers.

Going back to the example at the beginning of this chapter, it would be remarkably easy for any manager to stock hot sauce and call a repairman to fix a broken door. However, the manager needs to know that such things need to be done. Since the manager isn't physically delivering hot sauce or items from the refrigerator with the broken door, the manager must find a way to get that information. Similarly, if widgets don't fit or break frequently and if quality assurance machines require three to five attempts to confirm the quality of an item, that information must travel from the man turning the wrench to the person who can change the widgets.

Know When to Hold 'Em

Bottom line: As a leader, you need to develop a radar that tells you what information is critical. You need to listen to everyone, but not necessarily act on everything. You need to always listen for actionable items and correctly identify the items that require you action while simultaneously staying the hell out of the way when you're contribution simply undermines the team. Lead, follow or get the hell out of the way isn't just a platitude; it's a great guideline to follow. Pay special attention to the get the hell out of the way point. Consciously and intentionally decide when your team should act and not you and remove yourself from the equation; just don't remove yourself from the conversational banter.

With that marvelous detachment, you need to understand the view from the grip of the wrench turner, but you must experience this vicariously. See the world through the eyes of the employee to be able to accurately collect information regarding your company and your unit's function. This view must be able to connect those grassroots problems with grandiose vision. That's the value of middle management.

Then you have to summarize in 100 words or less what the grassroots employees need and why to senior leadership.

Chapter 10: Bluffing with BLUF

The BLUF brief is a sweet little tool from the military, but I'll wager it would work well in any sector. BLUF is bottom line up front. And it's a method used to communicate succinctly critical information on which you need senior leaders to take action.

The acronym is a misnomer, since you don't actually want to bluff about anything; you want to give it to them straight. Trouble is: senior leaders in all walks of life don't have time.

Here's an example:

```
BLUF:    Recommend    Changing    Widget
Contract
```

```
Background: For 20 years, we've been using
Acme  widgets  due  high  quality  and  low
failure  rate.  However,  a  recent  informal
study  showed  that  nearly  10%  of  these
widgets  don't  fit  our  bolts.  We  have
checked  with  other  branches  and  found  they
have  similar  problems  with  these  widgets.
```

```
Alternative Company A, $.02 per widget
Alternative Company B, $.04 per widget
Alternative Company C, $.07 per widget
Alternative Company D, $.09 per widget
```

Make Time to Write Short

I hope you already get the fact that an effectively written BLUF is a challenging task. Condensing a complex, possibly technical topic into a few dozen words that should be able to travel independent of any briefer who could answer questions is a major undertaking.

I trust you're already familiar with the Abraham Lincoln—ism: I'm sorry to write you such a long letter, but I didn't have time to write you a short one. Short writing is brain-busting brutal. You should write and re-write a BLUF. You should give it to colleagues and subordinates for editing.

When you send this red-star cluster up your chain of command – when you send this shot up to your leadership, make absolutely sure it is clear, concise and unquestionable. Take time so your senior leadership doesn't have to.